TIME FOR VERSES

Eduard Schmidt-Zorner

ISBN: 978-81-19228-41-6

First Edition: 2023
Rs. 200/-

Cyberwit.net
HIG 45 Kaushambi Kunj, Kalindipuram
Allahabad - 211011 (U.P.) India
http://www.cyberwit.net
Tel: +(91) 9415091004
E-mail: info@cyberwit.net

Printed at Replika.

Contents

DURING THE YEAR

Autumn Moon

Blossom and leaf know change and turn,
earth days see constant beginning and end;
hold the spark of eternal fire in hand,
smile at vanishing years,
ignore the tick of the clock,
take the staff and continue to walk
the road, the steep winding stairs.

People are scattered like leaves by storm.
World fires blaze, and death reaps on earth.
Preserve this flame of mysterious birth,
which knows no decay, only lasting desire,
whose agony is lost in blissful devotion.
From a flowering exuberant explosion
incense clouds of sweetness emanate.

Time dissolves easily, so full of sun,
drink from the scarlet chalice of this day.
Gently, the linden tree hangs an array
over us: its subtle green filigree veils.
Chimes, in the distance, sound,
hours like fluttering leaves fall to the ground
slowly on the counting weighing scales.

Darkish and solemn under bitter air
leaves rustle on the narrow path,
announcing early autumn days.
Sweetly suffused by ripe apples' scent,
trees stretch their bronze-golden branches.

Wine winds purple chains around walls,
so rich and ripe, so full, this summer's end.

Shining like last bouquets
embraces summer selves in final love,
whispers goodbye; the cooing of a dove,
the heavy perfume of saved hay,
silage, straw, cabbage, and apples,
of pumpkins and grapes;
sustenance for long cold winter days.

Late Harvest Moon

Through a greenish curtain shot a spark.
Now it is gone. What's bothering my heart?
Colourful summer burned to the ground,
sun-kissed in golden deaths.
A withered mound of humus found
to pave the path for flora's birth.

How may we walk so lost in thoughts
through tawny meadows' band?
Over us, free, untamed across
wide clouds of light expand.

And all around the pale, discoloured world
in a contemplative farewell stillness,
as if in every leaf impressed
a holy fate is silently fulfilled.

Footsteps sound through silent hours,
breathless, anxious. Moon stands bright.
Above us, waving, longing, drunken,
aurora borealis sheds its northern light.

Fallow Moon

Summer winds waft with heavy scents
through acacia's foliage crown,
with lilac, primrose fragrance blends,
a leaf comes loose and tumbles to the ground.
Summer flares off, like fire in a storm.
Wreaths wither, rot away, transform.
Midday blaze scorches now the garden,
armoured figures threaten, clandestine,
gigantic and grey, a wake for the sun
around the heaven's hem of silver shine.

A wrathful summer paces, thundering
night after night, through thirsty fields.
A dome above of lightning, blazing;
Below us, are illuminated, dark grey peaks.
Nights, when shooting stars begin to rain
sultry from the daytime pain,
wind-tossed treetops joining forces
like a herd of wild black horses.
Sweet-scented flowers on a darkish meadow,
dropping minutes vanish in their fragrance,
slow, like gentle honeydew.

August Evensong

Soft-winged breeze flows.
A woodlark sings.
Dusk spreads on undulating hills,
dew unites with winding rills.

Wafts from the sirens' singing
oscillate like sounds of late,
deep subconscious longing
gives us time to contemplate.

Crickets fiddle in the grass,
a creek runs through rough ground,
the roses glow in the garden,
gorse blooms along the paths.

From far, a jackdaw's scream,
then a long and heavy sigh,
as if the mountain takes a breath,
gusts are falling from high.

Buzzing through the treetops,
a swarm of rushing birds.
I hear from the beech slope
the wingbeats of a dove.

Shepherd and flock seek rest
near fields of corn abundance,
in orchard's fruited vines
still rests the summer silence.

On sylvan peaceful scene
the sun is shining brightly,
and stripes of light, lightly
turn the glade into a sundial.

The late summer's sun
rests on bare rock's face
to grant to moss and ivy
a last warm favor's grace.

Waiting for the reaping hook,
rich meadows' golden gift,
the austere, rough threshers' work
comes to its end.

Harvest celebrations fade
around the rich filled barns,
on the farmhouse's threshing floor
summer night drapes veils galore.

The opulent harvest time
is gone, green pollen wave
and dust of rye and wheat fields
are blown and flown away.

Scurrying through a picket fence,
from the stable to the shed
slips a marten's fleeting shadow
swiftly up the birch tree's stem.

From deep forests soothing silence,
when the silent star balls glow,

distant monotone night's song
of steady falling waterfalls.

Final strokes of nine
peal from a village tower,
the whining sound of a violin
over the dreamers hover.

Night Colours

Red, dispersed by the wind
Ten thousand petals
fall into the river...
are flames.
Fire in the green disarray.

My purple cry permeates into
the luminous power of the night,
rotten wood glows and bitter roses
bloom like your attentive lips,
thoughts true as the rain.

Dancing in cloudy waves,
gloomy violet of the evening.
Sun pressed into a formula,
insoluble in the whirl of reality.
Grey weaving, passionate.

The pale window-cross of the moon,
the blue light of the graveyards
shine in the puddles and
the barmy glow
reddens the pale gardens.

How blind they are,
the houses, the glistening streets,
how numerous they are
and narrow, exuberant,
those stone leaflets.

Voices in the Grain Field

I walked through pasture-loneliness,
through vast fields of grain.
Midday's sun is half covered by clouds,
which stretched their wandering shadows,
lingering over harvest-pale land;
I listened into the great silence,
which weaved over fields of wheat.

I hear verses in the distance.

A cloud shadow gently slid,
transparent, broad-winged, over fields,
with the shadow came a breeze,
that stirred the heavy heads of all the ears.
In a soft murmur with the waft of wind,
flew the voice from stalk to stalk,
until it lost itself in a distant whisper

I hear my ancestors speak.

Hay Moon's Morn and Eve

Mellow are the July nights,
when the sunset's reddish fading
and the early morning lights
dawning blur and blend.

When summer with red roses
bleeds to death so rapidly,
cawing ravens mourn the dead,
the blackbird has not sung
its last song yet.

Warm rays from the sunset
make distant peaks glow red,
the scream of the wild eagle
sounds over the forest silhouette,
while pale-cold falls the mist
into the closing day.

Under lime trees, under elms,
under thatched roof's hanging wings
overgrown with moss and weeds,
stretching wide and shielding.

I want to put it into a song
what on the moonlit village green
I heard the fairies lisping.
What grey stone's mossy green
inscription said to me.

Fog pictures rise in the twilight,
from the dark days 'past.
I hear faint voices whispering,
sounds of pleasure, lament, anger.
A last farewell, so distant.

Silent night in the deep forest
around the birches' black-white bark;
around the alder's trunks so dark,
flows the moonlight soft and mild.

Changing Moon

Summer, so soon,
wild strawberries grow
under a bright lamp
which is shining all night,
the full Strawberry Moon,
as signal and call
to harvest the ripening fruits.

July's full moon,
a month so full of light.
The summer flames up,
the wind wafts hot
through the crowns,
treetop replete with sunshine.
Singeing the barley fields
in the midday sun.

August blesses with raised hands.
Pollen rises like incense.
A solemn mood, full of awe.
Flowers' blossom will soon wither.
The willow hangs over the river.
The nights are sultry,
shooting stars fall, the air is still,
the asters sway in longing.

So sunmatt, rich and mature,
swells the ripe apples' smell.
In the cloud shadow, I rest,

so dreamdazed, sweet-inebriated.
Flaming on the hillside, the summer flees.
The reapers' song tune,
sustained by the sound of the sickle,
the steel crescent,
competing with the waxing moon.

Green shall remain the Earth

When the evening casts its grey net,
on the horizon
a strip of solemn pine appears.
The day sinks, the sun extinguishes,
as if it never existed.
Raptors' cries above the treetops resound,
the wide rye fields wave abound,
rooftops visible behind woodland,
rural silence floats to the rising stars
to mark the warm day's end.
Lost, remain the swampy lakeshores
around the boggy resilient grounds,
with reeds and tall sedge
at motionless water ponds.
An owl screams in the thicket,
a crake fills the clearing with its call.
Last dying rays over the slope
like a trinket.
The yew tree shields the graves
of Celtic cemeteries,
a dove coos,
sound of murmur in the sacred grove.
The hair, anointed with olive oil,
lush the mint, the laurel adorns the head.
Knotted black ivy hangs on the wall
in competition with wild wine and roses
the cypress stretches tall
I offer fragrant posies.

Summer Threshold

The morning comes with tangy air,
pulls bushes and trees out of the mist.
In the windbreak of the timber forest
deer fray the velvet from their antlers.
From the green sedge, the trunks shine red.
Jays make a noise in the thickening,
overgrown moor forests host brazen crows,
wanderlust of the grey geese,
lapwings stagger over the swamp meadows,
worried for their young, with plaintive cries.

Hidden in the reed bed of the riverbank,
a grey heron stands.
Lonely on one leg and contemplates.
From the nearby rye field,
the illusion of the smell of bread,
the air sings, and the earth listens.
No hunter's shot.
All is full of lust -
a summer without end.
The first heavy raindrops fall on my hand.

Unexpected

I bath my feet in the water
of a mountain stream,
who speaks gnome-like to me,
chatters and mumbles incessantly.
Willows hang their branches
into the foamy water,
as if surrendering,
powerless, sad, and tired.
Toads begin to spawn.
Butterflies tumble high.
The wailing cry of a buzzard in the sky.
The bark of a fox,
and hark,
a dog's responding bark -
Then a leaden silence,
like under a hood, a glass dome.
A quiet, so soundless.
Motionless.
Suddenly, a crackle, a breaking.
An old oak branch,
like a grey-brown snake,
crashes onto the path,
hits the ground with a dull sound -
the call of a pheasant hen.

Then it is quiet again.

Snow Moon

Wind from the north-west
grooms the wild lyme grass.
We observe the sky,
contemplate the moon's shine,
enjoy the crickets' choir,
they sing into the night.
To prevent a fall
your hand rests in mine.

Strawberry Moon

I look up from my book of poetry
and see your 'seek and hide' play.
You peek through the *Reeks*' valley
then rise like a released balloon,
let loose over the mountain range
on this night in June
and pour a silver glow
over the slopes and a lonely grange.

You are so close to us now
on your elliptical path.
So peaceful, so feminine, *Luna*.
Not like your wild brother *Sol*.
So round and full,
filling the sleeper's dreams.
Moving the ocean waves,
silently rocking the world
casting gentle shadows.

Forest Myth

The forest, familiarity confers,
holds many lives in disguise.
It is still wintertime, freeze.
Ice and snow transform trees
into bizarre shapes.
Soon, a mild wind wakes
the forest from wintry slumber.
Lively forest abode:
In the basement a pack of wild boars,
in the cellar a fox's den,
in the attic the wood grouse
with its black gown.

Spring moss, filigree sporophore,
scatters millions of spores.
In March, hazelnut blossoms,
open their pollen grain,
generate pollen rain,
subtle explosions.
Cones of conifers send their seeds
on an uncertain journey.
Love play in the wind,
pollen dust, gold stain.

Symphony of colours,
shapes and smells,
anemones attract insects
with their seductive scent.
Wild garlic promises taste,

indulgence, a stimulant.
Light controls the process,
warm are the sun's rays.

Bright day events change
with nightly shadow signs,
accentuated strange noises.
Thunderstorms are brewing,
rain is heavily pouring.
A toad runs away, puzzled,
a leaf on which a beetle sits,
is hit by a drop
the beetle flung away.

Then calmness settles.
Water evaporates,
steam clouds form
over the dense green.
Rich, fertile, odorous.

LIFE CYCLE

The Blessing of Forgetting

Burned into the ridges of the human brain,
this centre of emotions, memory, and pictures.
Data coming up like on a computer screen,
fragments imprinted in the mind, agglutinated pain,
distressing recollections or a pleasant rhyme;
some come to the surface, spring to mind,
stay monolithic, overshadow, influence the time,
those, mercifully submerged in oblivion, left behind.

Forgetting belongs to dough-like yeast.
If we could not forget, we would be slaves of the past.
Some of my mementoes are an ice-cold winter night
over dark steel factory outlines, a full moon – bright;
hand in hand with mother on empty streets,
streets lined by houses destroyed on war nights,
only left behind as crater chains,
a smell of decay, time-dust washed into the drains.

Living in ruins, streets like dentures with missing teeth,
my parents, and me as an additional package,
unborn, duty unpaid, in the coldest month of the year.
Bitter poverty, happy to have a crust of dry bread to eat;
I did not know anything else for two decades.

An empty tin as a birthday present, a wooden stick,
the little drummer, pa rum pum pum pum.
Dead hare on a balcony wall, from which blood dripped,

eyes staring, a questioning glance, illegally shot.

Rubble pours out of a ruined building
the guts spilt out of the dead cat on the debris,
lying on top of the broken bricks like a warning;
like a mourning of the dead, buried underneath, reduced to ash:
People who never came back to the light of the day.

Messed-up childhood, disturbed,
until the end of my time.
We never forget wounds, they never heal,
exposed to a haunting memory
which never fades away.

Healing

I grew up amidst ruins,
remember a dead cat, exposed
on the debris pouring out of a
lonely porch of a destroyed house.
Destruction everywhere, also in my heart
I had no toys, no space to play,
refugees we were, displaced people.

In a box, I found two tiny wooden blocks,
unfinished.
And I found a thimble.
And a wooden mushroom,
which my mother used to darn the socks.

I placed the blocks on top of one another,
and added the thimble as a turret,
gave the mushroom next to it
the order to stand straight
to serve as an umbrella to keep me safe
in the house, which I constructed.

Remaining Dreams

The graveyard of dreams
rests on cold dark days.
Frost rises on tree bark,
picks dry pinecones,
encircles me, like prey,
strips the leaves from branches,
which tumble down, on withered reeds.

I walk the path,
where sunken crosses stand.
When the sun is shining again,
let thoughts drift
past weeping willows,
who bend their heads
into shallow streams.

When remembering, the dead,
their dreams,
we see, what remained of them.

Calling Your Name

I never knew my grandfather,
never made his acquaintance
or felt his affection, his closeness.
I talk often to the dead,
try to share moments, explain my fears,
or to ask for their opinion.

I speak to them to make a connection.
Will they answer me from a distance?
Do they know my apprehension?
Hard to hear them in the noise
of this side's distracting diversions.

I imagine an old man with white hair
holding my hand, smiling,
as we walk through the streets,
lined with chestnut trees,
and pass through wheat fields;
he is talking to me or remains silent.

Silence is often an answer
to questions whose response
would be too elusive.
In this dream we have a dialogue:
he explains things to me
and I ask hundreds of questions
to discover an unknown domain.

We have now a conversation
between rows of graves,

where startled deer watch the living
who search for traces of the dead,
stand motionless on the clearing
of this peaceful location, so soothing,
that even the hind and the fawn
are surprised to hear the steps
on the carpetlike lawn.

I would have liked to listen to him,
to his experience and vast knowledge.
He suffered two wars,
survived the first and lost a son and a daughter.
He did not see the end of the second,
nor Hitler's death which he yearned for.
Nothing remained of him:
He not only lost his life.
He lost everything.

Only a handful of ashes is left
in a plot, one meter by one meter,
with a simple headstone.

I have a yellowed photo,
mounted on brown cardboard.
At the bottom, it says:
Atelier Raspe
Imperial court photographer 1894
an illegible address on the reverse side,
handwritten in gothic script.

His permanent address now is:
Central Cemetery,
field twelve, row eight, grave thirty.

Yellowed Memories

Snow-covered fields lie wide
on which playful crows are dancing.
Deep stretches the countryside
up to the frozen hem of the horizon
uniting with the Baltic Sea.
Drains and ditches, silver lanes,
willow trees, wizen.
A buzzard hovers over the plains.

A picture book takes childhood by the hand;
memories settle as dust on what remains.
Sun penetrates through roof beams
into an imaginary faded wonderland.
There it is, my island under dreams:
Endless *taiga*, abundant clouded lake land.

Would like to hide, seek shelter, in fields of rye,
or between those thumbed pages of a fairy tale,
star money coins like rosary beads recounting,
pass through my fingers, dreamily,
to pay for moonlight over the *Curonian Spit*
and the *Vistula* river.

The memory suitcase gets heavier,
heart grows old
a thousand nights since passed,
counted by falling calendar sheets,
the hair grows white, open fields are cold,
a broken cross warns at the waterside.

Only thoughts remain on yellowed photos:
A forlorn couple with me
in front of green pine forests.
A lonely house near marshy meadows.
The step beyond the horizon is not far away.

Parting

Clear and austere
stands the embracing air;
trees stretch their bronze-gold branches,
like suntanned arms,
wild wine like purple braids on walls,
prematurely falling leaves
rustle on the narrow path.
Sweetly suffused by apples' scent,
so rich and ripe this summer's end,
shining like last bouquets,
announcing early autumn days.

The wounds of life are burning,
no herb can ever heal.
Hard strikes the hand of death,
but lays to rest a tired man.
Sombre behind the treetops
fades the last afterglow.
Life's burden weighs heavily;
it almost seems to me
it's even easier to die,
finally.

Tarot Cards from a Drawer

I remember, there were shadows, which frightened me,
when I was a child, haunting figures, bogles, nightmares.
I looked for a place, where I could hide,
from fear, the unknown, threat, school, dogs, thugs,
the milkman, darkness, the banging door.
No corner to hide, not even a cupboard was our own.
I needed somebody to hold my hand,
to protect my heart,
to put my feelings into a safe place.
To keep my secrets safe
in the repository of my heart.
Light is shining through
the ice flowers of the attic window.
Light from a silver disc.

The Shot

I never walked this road
in earlier days,
behind the village,
through the brown-grey fields.

Laburnum mixes with tall reeds,
fallow deer leaves a trace in the grass,
outraged pheasants burr
wild ducks hearken.

A snail drags her house lonely
over a tractor track
imprinted in the mud.

In the silence, you hear
the rustling of the clouds.

Everyone awaits the hunter's shot.

Farewell Letters

Tempus fugit, as the Latin says,
"time flies" the vernacular repeats,
as a trickle through a sieve,
unstoppable as long as we live,
irretrievable it escapes.

I do not see time as running out,
more likely to evaporate,
its farewell note is light and airy,
spring is passing, greenish as a veil,
a thin cloth, a gentle waft,
covered with pollen, powdered
with flower dust.

Summer finds it harder to say *adieu*,
lies heavy on us like a hot sheet,
resists, refuses transiency
with opulence, bearing fruit,
it shows maturity.
Amid life,
we are embraced by death.
Summer is not ready to accept
the last rose,
the last breath.

Autumn makes it easier to say 'goodbye'.
Just as the falling floatleaves
are the rain of many letters,
and pages of a book,

where everything is written down,
like calendar sheets with aphorisms,
and bygone dates.

Winter leaves its farewell letter behind,
puts it on the table,
for everyone to see, to read.
Cold is the fire of the fireplace,
corpse-cold,
a plume of blue smoke rises,
bare of words the writing is,
everything has already been said
with frost, snow, and torpor,
the vanishing white,
the emerging black.
Grey is the envelope.

Prospect

I sit in the café and watch the pavement.
The street scene is particularly eloquent:
Pigeons and other birds
involuntary and uncomprehending
became witnesses of bypassers' journeys.
These patient beings raise their voices,
draw attention to stories of flight and displacement.
Those who would see me from the outside,
would find a disturbed ageing observer
of a patch-work world
who became stranded
in his search for a place of anchorage.
The rain is so depressing, and to add to it,
the suburban train rattles past.
A shopping list bobs on a puddle
like a lonely boat,
the food list is hardly readable anymore,
has become rather unimportant.
One wishes or hopes
that the day may be good.
"Have you had a good day?"
is the repeated question.
The cup in front of me has a Christmas theme:
Green, red, gold.
A piece of cake provides the illusion
of festive biscuits and evokes nostalgia
from a forgotten homeland
that became strange to me,
a fellow traveller of the others

who pass by.
We are all homeless.
You don't leave when you can look back
on something.
Longing is hereditary.

Your hand in mine

Wind from the northwest
grooms the coat of wild horses.
We observe the starry sky,
contemplate moon's shine,
enjoy the choir of crickets
which sing into the night.

Holding me to prevent a fall;
your hand rests in mine.

One Twenty-Three

Years ago, a clock had stopped
on a cold winter's day.
Since then, its hands stood still,
now it is always one twenty-three.
A big clock,
which no longer gives a drop of time.
where otherwise time trickles out,
the time has now run out.
In a world of automation,
such a state would be called
deadly stagnation.

A terrible senselessness,
a clock that no longer works,
hangs there, a symbol of a sick time.
Chronos has lost his appetite
and refuses to eat.
A persistently non-working clock
without a punch line.
Yet it tells the time,
albeit stagnant,
and always the same.
Only once in twelve hours,
it shows the right time,
only once it is precisely one twenty-three
without a chime.

Fulfils some meaning of its existence.
All clocks point correctly,

you just have to look at them
at the right moment, the right time.
That is how it is with love,
at certain moments
you have to believe in it.

Fleeting Moments, Volatile Feelings

I sit at a table in front of a café in Paris
on the pavement, by the side of the road,
in the first row like on a terrace,
on a drab Saturday morning:
It looks like I hold an audience
because people slow their steps,
approach, nod, and wish me a good day,
some smile and continue their way.
people pass, some hurry,
or saunter off, the car traffic hums by.

A Romani woman stops
to read my future, she offers
good predictions from my palm.
I stay calm
I know it is utter superstition,
but I let her read the lines,
find an interpretation.
And she tells me
that I will find the great love:
The old story, I shrugged it off
because I had found it already
thought she was joshing me.

A newspaperman with a raucous voice
loudly exclaims the headlines.
I buy a copy and read the news,
which are grim and sombrely
and augur ill, sound portentous.

A friend pulls back the chair,
sits down at my table,
leans back with a sigh,
a poet, well known and able,
his black hat on his head,
from his mouth dangles a cigarette.

He takes a book from his pocket
and reads in German
a poem, written by *Goethe*:
'The gods give everything, the infinite ones,
To their beloved, completely,
Every pleasure, the infinite ones,
Every suffering, the infinite ones, completely.'

"Are you one of those the gods loved?"
I ask with a trifle hesitation.
He responds with a sad look:
"In my life, I have always suffered
more than I have rejoiced.
He closes the book.
A poet has to suffer,
life imposes grief,
and his heart blood
gathers like rain in a leaf
that is curved like a hand
to form a verse, a stanza,
words that run like sand.

Lonely Under Bridges

When after the chime at midnight
a homeless prepares his bunk,
spreads a worn blanket
and the decreasing lights of Paris
shine for rich and poor alike,
but not equally dispersed,
no 'equality' sets in,
and 'fraternity' only nests under the bridge
when the bottle is shared or circled,
goes from hand to hand,
from mouth to mouth,
mouths mute and bitter.
At the bridge pillars
the sky of the night breaks into halves.
It is better to stay awake
to take, dare, a nap during the day
in the *Parc de Bercy*
and think back
with nostalgic reminiscence
on times gone by,
when one comfortably got out of bed,
got into the car and drove to work,
accepted and respected,
until it all disappeared in a flash,
all became past, all gone.
It is lonely under the bridges.

Loss

Everything will pass.
We are marked by loss
by transience,
the loss of time
then follow in sequences
the various stages,
the loss of people, things,
the loss of grandparents, parents,
one's own age group, friends,
we lose eye sight, hearing, memory,
hair and beauty...

One becomes aware
that one is finite,
that one is passing away,
slowly disappear.

So, be attentive,
don't pay attention to the little pains,
one dies of many things,
not of lovesickness,
Life is full of sorrows
and worries.
That too will pass.
Only what you put on paper,
prose, poetry, literature,
will not be lost for ever.

Blunt Words Flee

So far
the glittering life has not blinded me
and obscured my view.
I see
clearly in the bright glow.
Although walls are being built again,
the cold has not yet taken over.
But they point to the sinking ship
at the entrance to the saving port.
I lie fortified on the other shore
and see an inflation of words
who have no weight.

We are all lying in trenches,
looking at each other
within nose's distance,
the clay of the battlefield
and death before our eyes.
We watch a supposed enemy,
who is behaving in the same way.
Cheated of our lives, lied to, betrayed.

Eternal Cycle

When the smell of decay,
already
clings to a death-doomed,
this ominous smell,
auguring farewell,
the end of time travel,
putrefaction
like old, withered wreaths
on graves,
wilting flowers for the recycle
and nature's circulation,
like withering, fungaled trees.

Earth to earth, dust to dust,
matter to the soil,
while energy somehow floats
in intermediate worlds
not knowing if those ethereals perceive,
watch or simply have found rest,
a silence they had longed for,
walking in nature, invisible
but near, among us,
with a view of the mountains,
the lakes,
so familiar to them,
the approaching waves of the sea,
or looking over the shoulder of a poet
whispering ideas into the ear,
which are absorbed
and woven into a living poem.

INSIGHTS

Shelf Life

In shelves full of wishes,
insights waited
between milk bottles
and daily news
scattered between doubts
and secrets
filled with hope and meaning
covered
with warning signs
concealing
the full hour's strike.

A busy crane lifts
every working day
into the neon light
of reckoning and settlement,
which shines into the smile of
achievers rushing by.

Day changes his shade,
night rehearses darkness.
Thoughts, monotonous
as a spinning wheel,
tumble into torn cobwebs,
held by knotted luck.

No stars fall into your hands
to rest from time walking.

The wind has ceased,
keeps silent,
behind walls, on streets.
We are an island
of our own,
in a sea of adverse impulses.

Our luggage waits
in a nearby train station.
We hear steps approaching.

Artist's Wellspring

Brush flits across the canvas,
paint knives cross it and spatulas,
the pallet becomes a painting.
Mixed paint is changing,
retrieved in the image again.
The frame waits.

Imprison not the mystery.
No linear structures, the straight line
is undivine, not nature's,
it confines.

Artistic work is exhaling, inhaling impressions.
A foray into new territory with vivid expressions,
every glance, every stroke of the brush.
A frenzy, rush.

Allusions, shape, and material
make motives ethereal.
Sketch the skeleton, paint the skin, colour the soul.
I am a composer, painter, committed to colour,
artwork, my final result.

Woodcut weeps chips and splinters,
a wooden board prepared with care,
smooth like cat hair, injured by sharp iron,
furrows are engraved,
a burin, exposing deep layers.

A woodcut emerges by cutting and carving.
There is no return, no healing.
What remains matters,
a triumph of the knife.

Unlike in etching, when metal is scratched,
acid dictates the digestive process
to bleed ink into handmade paper
to show the progress.

Everything is handicraft.
Work of the hand,
art makes us free.

Unsolved Mystery

Aren't they wonderful, these tunes
of *Chopin's Nocturne Opus 9 No. 2* ?
Piano music resounded from a window
when I walked down
a cobblestone covered road,
years ago in *Warsaw*.

This music filled the space
between old houses,
facades that are flaking,
echoed from wall to wall,
hovering sounds,
tunes like dragonflies,
volatile and floating.

I could visualize the light hands
sliding over the ivories.
Notes stringing together,
then dissolving, dancing,
taking shape and blossoming,
etherifying.

Who could model
notes and octaves
and give them life and soul?
To let a symbol become C sharp
or D-sharp for a harp
or fis or ges, a physical frequency.
Many things remain a mystery.
Some forever.

Conjecture on a Water Plant

Reed bent by a breeze,
a thinking reed,
thinking so deep
riverbanks so steep,
streamlets gush,
bluish-green rush,
bulrush,
bluerush, blue so blush,
fields so lush, full of hay.
At first blush - a silent day,
quiet cozy bowers,
pouring rain showers
hush little thrush!
Lizards hide
under sun-heated stone crush
at the wayside
greenblack, attentive, plush.

We pick fruits in
orchards, in the garden,
we harvest the wine
in wicker baskets
to keep the grapes.
We sort the apples,
sort pears and beans
we brush, clean the yard,
the leaves away.
The cooper seals with rushes
barrels full of grape blood

which splashes in goblets,
casks.
A bath in the lake to refresh.
Wood sedge, reed, and rush.
Ducks in their habitat dabble.
High in the sky,
an eagle eyes its prey
in the reedbed,
but it escapes.
An otter dares its way through the cane.
Autumn day closes its gates.

Overhead

Overhead power lines
stretch like cobweb threads
across the pale horizon,
the seemingly endless sky,
they transport traces
of dreams, statements,
scraps of words, laments,
through the emptiness,
the grassy plains,
along boreal forests,
over a stark frozen landscape.

In the ear, fragments of words,
sentences, sighs
they flow away like sand
in an hourglass
some settle or fade,
dissolve or pulsate,
strand.
Hours drip like drops
from a leaking tap
monotonous.

Lost words return
and turn against the speaker.
The sound mocks the images
that emerge like chimeras.
Tomorrow
tears will be the counting unit,

curses and accusations
your time-measuring devices.

Your words stay close to my heart.
No star falls into your street
to rest or to fulfil wishes.
Presence is a knot of happiness
and I pick my day apart,
like a flower, to ask
does she love me, does she not?

The antient watchmen of the night
have clothed themselves in iron.
Stride in circles towards the light.
Traces of the plain still obscured,
horizons not yet conquered.
Twilight hides them
in the sound of strings.

The Round Earth

When I think that the earth is round
that the other stars have a similar shape
spherical or a similar form,
like a potato or a ball in outer space:
Sun, moon, and stars,
Jupiter and Saturn, the red Mars,
perhaps formed by the big bang,
in the shape of aerosols,
splashing in all directions.

The thought of it amuses me.
Someone had a weakness
for round things,
Impractical though, monotonous,
and a waste of space
because spheres cannot be stacked.

If the earth would be a disc,
simply flat like a pancake,
everything would be easier,
no immediate risk,
a clear beginning and end,
instead of an endless,
theoretically, eternal,
trot around the globe
with no real hope
of a defined destination.

Again, in addition,
such an absurd idea,

to create these useless people
who destroy nature, fauna, and flora
and with their heads down in Australia
get headaches and are bitten by snakes.

A plate, as nice as the Netherlands,
clear and smooth, far-sighted.
At least on Sundays,
you can see on the horizon
who is coming for coffee, a visitation,
and whether warriors are sneaking up
with bad intention.

The deceased are thrown over the edge,
overboard, into the darkness of the universe.
And it is easier to commit suicide,
environmentally friendly anyway,
a clear end.

One might ask,
what does it look like underneath
the mysterious disc
It would make sense
if nothing was there.

One could also distribute seas,
oceans and mountains more sensibly,
also, remove day and night,
since sleep
is just an unproductive waste of time
because in the middle of the night
one ponders
about the physical form of stars.

Shouting Across to the Far Shore

Shouting truths to opposite shores,
suspecting someone to hear the words.
Letters and syllables get caught in the thorns,
arrive garbled and incoherent, torn,
and misunderstood,
wander into other ears,
are printed on paper,
plagiarized,
and appear as headlines
exclaimed by the street vendors,
spat out onto the pavement
faint remnant
of public opinions
until decayed and weathered
crushed under the feet of minions,
ground by the rack and pinion
of approaching times.

Again

Again, one of those sleepless nights
when books become cushions
and memories haunt the minutes
which are sheep in other nights
and are unable to be counted
with all the thoughts
foreboding shadows
and expectations,
desires.
Morpheus the god of sleep,
the son of *Hypnos* and his brother
Phantasos
play jokes with mortals,
and turn the hourglass,
provide more time
for night watches
and pain.

LOVE

Found

A soothing night
covers a humming metropolis,
it blankets the quarters,
its banlieues.
Lone men and women,
alone among millions,
lost, in a sea of lights,
and night-shaded streets.

I found a counterpart,
and hold her hand.
Smells and taste of vanilla, herbs,
I discover oases and hills,
valleys with all their secrets.

I play with her on mystic strings,
unlock unknown sounds
which ether away,
fade like the melodic clink
of piano tunes
conjured by ivories.

Your breath in my ear,
words whispered into your hair,
we sink into love,
and drown
in a warm embrace.
Your lips entice me

to kiss ripe fruits
from cherry branches.

Attar, made
from the essence,
of roses, herbs, and spices.
A drop on your lips
a drop on my skin.
You are like the wine
from the *Languedoc*
a taste on the tongue,
overwhelming, floral, ripe,
with a taste of the autumn sun.

For Baroness M.

It seems to me
that I met You once,
thousand years ago.

I think it was
between *Euphrates* and *Tigris*
or as stardust in space,
flying past each other.

Or long before the time in the taiga.

Souls, not yet sedentary,
hovered over the Baltic Sea,
destined
to meet again one day,
to talk about mysterious premonitions
which inherent experiences
obscurely whisper to us.

I see the familiar now differently,
feel strange thoughts,
follow ideas and traces.

Maybe I will find
a way to you again,
that I never dreamed of?

Zahra – Rose

Black tropical rain forest,
smells and taste of vanilla, herbs,
discovering oases and hills,
valleys with all their secrets.

I play with you on bitter strings
unlock unknown sounds
which ether away like music,
fade like the cling of piano tunes.

Your breath in my ear,
words whispered into your hair,
we sink into love and drown.
Your areolas enticed me
to kiss ripe cherries from branches.
I leaf through shrivelled petals.

Perfume, scents,
pressed from roses.
A drop on your lips
a drop on my tongue.
You are like wine
from the Kabyle mountains
called *désir*
with a taste of shale.

Rose of the Maghreb,
your skin has the tint
of burnt-orange rock
like the Atlas highlands.

The hall of lost steps

I remember as a child
the sounds of footsteps,
when I sat under our table.
I watched shoes, feet, socks,
moving, passing by,
walking away, returning
shuffling to and fro, finally pausing
for a rest.
The sound of lost people
and their lost steps.

I took shelter under the table,
no desire to see faces.
I heard voices and different languages,
serious talk,
weeping, shouting, arguing.
That was captivating, more interesting
the connection 'foot – voice'
was more revealing.

Even today I listen to the sound
of feet on the ground.
Recognize people I know
by the sound of their steps
and the sound of the voice.
Faces say nothing
they are part of the stage,
feign feelings, emotions
are masks,
interchangeable.

Incomplete

Found old letters in a drawer,
like rustling, heaped, dry leaves,
which, letter by letter,
lead into serious realms,
a few were a laugh,
some encouraging and revealing.
They reflected a futile, perishable past.

Metaphors cheaper by the dozen.
Story beginnings, relationship endings.
Short stories with sad content,
curses and songs of hate,
long-sought-after rhymes and verses,
carved, pressed into white pages.

Concise irreversibility, final lines.
Sentences cut amidst by sharp blades.
Pages with many spots of tears.
Some letterheads in pink or purple
or smelling of violets.
One with traces of red lipstick on it.

I also found letters from me.
Unfinished, inconclusive,
in a state of limbo, indecisive,
broken off and never sent,
never mailed, forgotten legacies.

Stammering of words of love,
sound trivial when read today,
sweet talk, a little bit of levity,
platitudes, nothing of depth -
as fire now in the fireplace,
substitute for the heat,
which was never mediated,
never has been transmitted.

Friendship Test

Place your friendship on weighing pans
and watch how the pan reacts.
Put the friendship on a scale.
See the direction the scale-pan takes.
Hold friendship in your hands
and feel its weight.
Put it to the test
and see where the pointer tends.

Subject it to an endurance test
push it to its wear resistance.
Candle it like an egg.
Apply a standard,
measure the length and width.
Do a viscosity test,
follow the way of the falling ball,
its depth,
the tenacity to prove the strength.

Forget it all.
Reach out your hand.
pull your friend
towards you,
and give him an embrace.

Notes of Times Gone By

I met her in *Gorky Park*
on a Sunday afternoon,
a day with minus 10 degrees,
it became dark, soon
icy winds from the taiga blew,
trees were covered
in heavy snow.

It flew over a spark,
and lit my heart.
We met every day
in the park
we shared the same way,
went hand in hand
in full harmony
hoped that there
would be no end.

Sat in the venerable library
of the *Lomonosov* University,
and stuck our heads,
cheek to cheek,
into many books
and read *Lermontov*,
empathised with writers,
felt the desperation
of *Fyodor Dostoevsky*,
and saw our reflection
in the verses of *Pushkin*.

PAST AND STILL PRESENT

On that Night

As the dawning blue shadows grow
on Albanian's mountainside,
walking down the Appian way
with a heavy gait,
leaning on a stick,
a white-haired woman.

Down in a hamlet,
a blind man is counting chimes,
stands in awe, silent, under the heaven.
Shepherds on brown fields,
throw down their staffs and run in horror.
"We have seen the mother of times".

Her last word was the first,
written with a brush
on your forehead.

Flowers and buds know change.
Stars and moon witness beginning and end.
Peoples are blown away,
traceless, invisible like leaves,
swept by the storm night and day.
World fire is blazing, and Death reaps.
Scythe's sound of steel.
Dark veiled in a narrow lane
messengers of *Hades* conceal
men, who are slain.
Voices call me without mouth,
mute jaws
and an oath of revenge.

During the Blitz

Waiting in the dark, we dream of light;
deep, underground, we hear detonations,
vibrations of bombing causing fright,
impact of loads dropped on a town.

What awaits us outside is unknown,
when we inch to daylight (which we desire):
a day darkened by smoke,
or a night glowing with fire?

Grasped by fear and helplessness,
by air raids and trembling walls,
recognising nightmare's relentlessness
in the horror of today's sundown
when night falls like a gown
and sirens sound the all-clear,
in these days of war and fear,
in shelters with neighbours and strangers.

Wherever we look into dark future's night,
far from the here and now, flickering light,
far from home, hoping, and hearing
the word without knowing its meaning.

Did we see warnings looming up?
Signs on the wall, in *Belshazzar*'s hall?
Did we anticipate tyrants, invasion, depravity?
Victims, the dead, the bombs on Coventry?

Sons of the land clothe themselves with death,
arm themselves to kill their own kind
in the places of horror, up and down the land.
Dream weavers weave a wreath,
money counters count and pay in kind;
armourers forge, steel unsheathed;
soldiers kill; leave thousands bereaved:
we are all led like puppets on a string.

In the city of lost angels,
a masked man sharpens his black scythe,
saddles his mighty horse
for the very last fight.

Burn, Phoenix, that your ashes bear fruit,
keep your heart's blood, Pelican, to feed us.
Grim Reaper has his harvest time.
We hear graveyard bells chime.

Almost filled is the hour-counting shadow glass;
nearly faded, are pottery shards with your name,
the Tree of Life, standing pale in the rain;
wilted, the rosebush that lived your love,
windblown breath that carries your words,
naked, featherless - lonely peace dove.
Go where you have never been before,
where yet so many wait.

Drowned in the Danube

On the embankment of the Danube,
in front of the Hungarian Parliament,
stand sixty pairs of iron shoes,
pointed towards the river,
a sad ornament
making hearts quiver.

20,000 were brutally killed
along the banks of the Danube,
forced to remove their shoes
to face their executioners
before they were slaughtered
without mercy in the early day,
falling over the edge
to be washed away
by the freezing waters.

Sixty pairs of 1940s-style shoes,
true to life in size and detail,
sculpted out of iron, so real,
a memorial simple yet chilling,
depicting the shoes left behind by
those murdered by the Arrow Cross,
fascist orders fulfilling.

The style of footwear –
a man's work boots,
a businessman's loafer,
a woman's pair of heels,

tiny shoes of a child,
standing there
in a casual fashion,
as if the people
just stepped out of them;
little statues, a grim reminder
of souls who once occupied them.

That winter,
men, women, children,
voices of pain afar,
fell into the Danube –
one after the other -
on their coats
the Yellow Star.
At that day the Danube,
a grave the riverbed,
was neither blue nor grey,
but red.

World in Fire

Red sun, pale moon,
black stars, omen of doom.
Storm tossed world,
times in a waft of mist, hurled.
Banshees washing blood-stained clothes
when people die in battles.

Under kettles… burning embers,
smouldering bonfire of nature,
which remembers lost empathy.
On the swords, dried blood, portending evil,
harvest, eaten by weevil, dour, ugly warriors.
A red coloured horizon in frantic fire.
Wood heaped for an eternal pyre.

Moving times of wrath
choking the throat, in temper,
clenching a rough fist full of resentment,
drowning in blind anger.
Searching a hand, which is offering liberation,
shelter and happiness
in the bleak empty times of loneliness,
which fill me with sorrow and horror,
which deny a horizon, a tomorrow,
blocking our paths in a brazen way,
preventing us to climb to heights,
to the light of day.

So that a beam strikes us and lights up our life
lifts us out of the darkness, a sharp knife
to cut the strings,
weaving eternal ropes around us.

Place de la Revolution?

The city of the revolution
no matter how free
sees assassination
secular society
fraternally or sisterly
now intimidated, angry
betwittered and facebooked,
charlied and flicted,
tumultuous and telepathic
disturbed and media-orientated
assailed by January
overwhelmed by uncertainty
people in sorrow marching
mute numbness in the banlieue
the free are masoning,
others are arguing
the powerful are building a human wall
in an empty street
fooling the world, which looks perplexed
so is Paris
in the today, vexed.

Leningrad Symphony

(On 9th August 1942, Karl Eliasberg gave a premiere performance of Dmitry Shostakovich's Seventh Symphony in besieged Leningrad)

Tree bark boiled to soup,
book glue was eaten.
Icy winter, men, frost-beaten.
The face of the town stands out
like a death mask under a shroud.
The Germans' siege of Leningrad.
November 8, Hitler's instruction:
"*Leningrad must die of starvation.*"

Rats, pets, and corpses
as food substitute.
River *Neva* frozen in ice,
Lake Ladoga, an ice shield,
a small loophole in or out,
over this icy bridge
seeking safety by evacuation
bringing help for the population.

The sad accounting of death,
bare figures, one and a half million perished,
no last flowers, no prayer, no wreaths
half a million buried
in the *Piskarevskoye* cemetery,
more left buried under the snow
a cold obituary.

Cholera, epidemic typhoid fever,
start spreading among the defenders.

Do you hear the children cry?
Do you see them die?
Bodies are pulled on sledges to the morgues.
Others were dropped at the side of the roads.
Funerals, graves, coffins could not be provided,
the number of mortalities too high.
A tidal wave of death that could not be contained.
Families, friends, and neighbourhoods disappeared.

A town encircled
by wild merciless animals
which cut off the lifeblood,
a vision of last judgement.
Leningrad, day, and night, bombarded
over 872 days was the city devastated.
Though bombs destroyed all food supplies,
those enclosed were determined to survive,
to withstand fascism, to fight for their lives.

Music was broadcast to keep up the spirit.
Performers and personnel
worked despite the bombshell
without compensation.
In the Leningrad radio
at rare times
when no music was broadcast
as a sign of life,
like heartbeats, the ticks of a metronome,
placed before the radio microphone
to assure that the resistance continued.

Into the mind of many
this rhythm was burned deeply.

Under this gloomy, oppressing cloud
Shostakovich finished his 7th Symphony,
while people died at six thousand per day.
He intended to defy the enemy through music,
with the weapon of notes, of composition.

Shostakovich's handwritten instruction was:
"*Dedicated to the heroic people of Leningrad.*
All instruments must play their part!"
Karl Eliasberg was appointed conductor.
He created an orchestra composed of survivors,
to perform despite starvation and dystrophy,
with violins, woodwind instruments, and brass
in a starved city,
strangled - short of breath.

Eliasberg procured a list of musicians,
twenty-five crossed out with black ink,
means: dead already…
Those known to be alive
were marked in red,
the colour of life and blood.
A drummer collapsed on the way to rehearsal,
the leading violinist died from starvation.
The rest unable to hold their instruments
longer than ten minutes
with their cold hands.
Hollow-cheeked *Eliasberg*
conducted his orchestra sitting on a chair
Bolshoi Philharmonic Hall under an icy canopy,

but civilians and defenders of the besieged city
were able to hear the powerful music.

In Leningrad, all were listening.
A great joy, a feeling of hope...
everywhere the concert could be heard.
Even by the enemy…
Marshal Zhukov kept "eighty minutes of silence,"
when his soldiers interrupted the fight
against the Germans
not to disturb the performance.

Strength lies in the prophecy
to conquer the clenched evil
by sound, melody, harmonic vibrations.
They never gave up.
The concert helped to support them,
encouraged them,
when they struggled to survive.

After the concert
which filled the hearts with confidence,
trust, and determination,
Eliasberg was presented with flowers,
by unknown souls.
From where did they come
in a town without a blade of grass?

Music's victory over barbarism,
the Russian soul, invincible,
strong, nourished by culture,
staying power and perseverance.

Built on Quicksand

When the sky frightens by emptiness,
we look for signs in the sand.
I took a handful of sand into my hand
and put it in my pocket
as a matter of foresightedness.

There are different kinds of darkness
where you can bumble around
or try to escape or have a ride
on a merry-go-round
to end in a notorious cycle.

There is also night blindness
or the dead phone, the deadline,
unanswered letters, unopened emails.
The ropes have been cut
the life drifts away.

Everything stays in its place,
but nothing casts a shadow.
'*Schlemiels*' in a row.
Everyday things solidify.
Like people who freeze in fright.

Motionlessness everywhere.
The reality, the presence,
an undefined sum of infinity.
Presence is the weakest,
rots and disintegrates the fastest.

Matter disappears
black absence of light remains.
The downside of reality,
which frays over the edges
demands its rights as a prodigal son.

It is all leaden disinterest and lethargy
as on a warm summer morning.
So, everything stays the same.
In this forgotten, eroding outhouse,
saw matter in the final stages of decay.
In final abandonment
time had infiltrated everything,
and decomposed it from within.
Thus, the misty presence
becomes past almost painlessly.

We may all be long dead
without knowing,
on an endless loop of immortality.
Or will things end somehow,
like breakfast, a book, a cigarette?

Where are all those we have lost?
The dead, the abandoned, the forgotten,
world crumbs, hopes, memories?
Nothing alleviates the current cruelty
of hopelessness and irredeemability.

There will be nothing left,
just this yellowed image
of a human footprint,
until it finally disappears
ends in this sand, this quicksand.

Quest for the Self

A glance behind the pain barrier,
to see if there is more
than a creature bent in self-pity
amidst a thorny hedge,
a prince sleeping in a castle
or yet the court jester
waking at the death bed...

Night Vigil

Night vigil of shadows
in another parallel world,
outside our own curtains
obscured, hidden, and disguised
Night vigil, evening mass,
held in darkness,
flickering candles, catafalques, and biers,
rolling hearses with the dead,
hollow-cheeked figures with extinguished eyes.
Curses, imprecations, evil deeds,
lie on the surface like water lilies on a lake,
reaching out for the living,
who are not aware of them.

In dark alleys that hate the light
moves mist over the wall,
nebulas ascend.
Obscure are the lanes
where problems fester
behind dimly lit windows.
Problems that drive to despair
and rob the breath, the lifeblood,
drive into death.
Where black ravens,
Those ghosts in disguise,
try to shift their torment onto others
to make their own stone
around their own necks
seem to weigh lighter.

Forge Peace

Top of Form
They still wait
for the right time to sow,
ploughshares stand ready,
to divide the soil into furrows,
even and parallel,
the sun stands low.
They face dark times,
times of grief and sorrow.
Wait hesitant, idle,
as steel storms rage
not far away.

Is it worthwhile
to till the field,
to tend the land,
plan for a yield
as on the wide horizon
gunfire and bombs
light up the nights?
The cannons bark,
the tank tracks rattle,
shelling on cities
missiles leave their mark.

The will to plant the seeds
and hope for a rich harvest
sinks.
People will die on the fields,

the soil their graves,
their blood will fertilise
the humus,
the plough remains
in the shed, unused,
a horse scrapes the floor in the shed,
the full seed basket,
next to an open casket;
the birds have a feed.

ploughshares became swords
again
instead to forge the swords
for good
into a peaceful tool.

Blinding Light

We light candles to commemorate,
to remind us of people or events.
We light lights to send admonition,
to set a signal, to trigger a reflection.

These flames also do us good,
They make us feel at home.
bring a pleasant feeling, a good mood,
a relief, a kind of disculpation...

Or we light candles
want to express expectation,
prepare ourselves for more light.
During the year we light
scented candles, wax candles, red or white,
show the colours of many a national flag.

Now, far away, at the edge of a forest,
in the borderland,
we perceive the red blaze of violence.
Flames burst from roof trusses.
Wheat fields, villages, forests burn.

The crowd of fleeing people
no longer resemble, are far removed,
from the vigils back in our cities,
where one man held the sign
NEVER WAR AGAIN

over his head,
plaintively.

That was long ago and is now forgotten,
the candles too.
Now destructive flames
call for reflection and reaction.

Too late,
the glow of mild candlelight
had blinded us.

Futility

Suddenly you realise
that you have to break with the past
because the past breaks you
in the long run,
the suffocating images at nights,
memories cast long eerie shadows
taint the air, befoul the present,
a miasma creeps from crevices
like poison gas.

Autumn leaves fall off trees,
but you cannot shake off the past
like the wind the foliage.
It comes in dreams, in spasms,
accompanies you,
is always at your side,
strides with big steps,
laughs scornfully in your face.

I want to turn my back
to trauma and memories
for good, a final act,
before it casts a shadow
on my casket and my grave
and burdens them.

Delete, erase, overpaint,
wash off, scrape off,
bring items to the waste.

But all in vain,
wanted to begin a clean slate,
but the past clings to me
like a limpet.

OTHER HORIZONS

Venice's Twilight

The waves lick at flaking walls
lower their voice, dreamily,
because the sun sinks soon
over the *San Michele* cemetery
like a tired, shrivelled, balloon.
Grey gives roofs a monotone shade,
provokes the sunset
to illuminate with manifold flames
that gild the rocking waves.
From *Santa Maria Assunta* call bells.

Around tree-lined squares,
resound my steps
in the maze of narrow alleys.
The setting sun lets facades shine.
It is time to serve supper,
to fill the glasses with wine,
like a ritual,
to taste sweet-sour sardines,
or prawns with polenta,
steaming and fragrant,
mixed with the reminiscent scents
of the *Ghetto Vecchio*,
of *zuppa di pesce* and *risotto*.
And the walls sigh
because they want to tell, to share
their memories, their moments,
like a dealing of playing cards

for a game of chance,
a chance that failed.

Somnolence overcomes me.
The soporific whisper of the waves,
sent from the lagoon, the *Grand Canal*,
triggered by gondolas and hurrying boats,
that transport feelings,
sail past, rowed with sure balance,
along hidden, enchanted gardens
that hide between palazzos and palazzinos.
Velvety light throws silhouettes,
the melodies of *Verdi* sound from windows
I feel the history of this place.
The clapping of the waves quietens,
as if the early morning, the pink dusk,
regulates the melodies,
or because the renewing rays of the sun
take over the senses, beguiling,
glad
that the heavy dreams of the night
are erased, wiped off the slate of time
and the smell of coffee from the *campo*
intoxicatingly seduces, accelerates
the heartbeat of Venice.

Rome

When I walk under a clear blue sky
along the *Tiber* to *Trastevere*
to imbibe and try
delicate culinary wonders
in the many cafes and bistros
of the colourful quarter
and attach my eyes
to the umbrella pine trees
on the horizon
not to succumb to dizziness
caused by the city's overwhelming beauty,
and when I hear
on the opposite side of the river
in the *rione XI - Sant'Angelo,*
the ancient wisdom whisper
from the walls in the alleys
of the *Ghetto Ebraico*,
then solemn peace flows into my heart,
that makes the cobblestones
feel like a carpet carrying me gently,
and with closed eyes, I feel the spray
of the *Trevi* fountains on my face,
when the hum of the cars,
which circle
around the equestrian statue
of *Vittorio Emanuele*,
changes to the melodic sounds
of the Italian tongue,
transformed into poetry, verses
and word fragments,
I become one with this city.

Istanbul

You turned colourless,
became faded.
Old pictures
promised me memories.
The sounds are still in my ear,
flapping wings of the pigeons
on the *Taksim* Square,
prayers from the minarets,
when life in the city begins.
The smell of the spices
from the street markets.
But the pictures disappeared
behind the borders of the frame.
when walls start to block the view
and oppression creeps in.

Inner Mongolia

Star-sprinkled, speckled
sky dome over icy ground,
snow dust covered.
Frozen rain clings to fir branches.
There is no light nor sound
only green veils of northern lights.
Flurries of snow over grey mountains
which have no paths or passes.
Horses graze on sediment pastures,
scrape food with their hooves
from under the snow layer.
Yaks give fat milk, patient animals.
Butter is beaten by tribal women
in their yurts near the fire.
In iron pots mutton meat boils.
Soon the sun will lure the first sprouts.

Sacred stone heap with a pole,
supplications on paper strips,
a silk scarf flutters as sacrifice.
A shaman hums incantations.
Any sense of time disappears
in meditation, a fearless beauty
surrounds and nourishes me,
whispers at treetops.

Snow melts with rising floods
changes rivers' course.
Torrential currents transform,

and create new tundra images,
re-paint the landscape
on a grey canvas, in a steel frame
of high clouds.
Eternal continuous change.